Vin Gupta, Chairman & CEO

Dear Customer:

Twenty-seven years ago, I came to this country with $50 in my pocket. And 22 years ago, I founded American Business Information, Inc. with $100 and a belief that small businesses needed an accurate, affordable source for sales leads and marketing information to help grow their businesses.

Today, we are a publicly-traded corporation with sales in excess of $75 million and over 600 employees. How did we do it? By practicing the same marketing concepts as presented in this book. These concepts really do work! And they are easy for anyone to understand and implement. You don't need to be a Rhodes Scholar or have a Harvard MBA! After all, Sam Walton of Wal-Mart never went to college, and used the same common sense approach to build a multi-billion-dollar corporation.

Our goal for this book is to share our marketing strategies with our 400,000 customers and millions more who are not our customers yet. It is your loyalty that has made us successful. And so, we want to share our proven methods to help you grow and prosper. We can't promise instant riches, of course -- there really is no easy money. But if you follow the basic concepts in this book, you will be successful in growing your business.

And when you do, give me a call and tell me about it. I love to hear "success stories" from customers. After all, that's what we're here for!

With kind regards,

Vinod Gupta

P.S. If you have any questions or need help, please call our office and one of our staff members will be glad to help you.

American Business Information®

5711 So. 86th Circle • P.O. Box 27347 • Omaha, NE 68127
Phone: (402) 592-9000 • Fax: (402) 331-1505

TABLE OF CONTENTS

I. INTRODUCTION: What is Business-to-Business Marketing?
   Challenges Facing Business-to-Business Marketers.....*2*

II. THE FIRST STEP IN MARKETING--KNOW YOUR CUSTOMERS!
   How to Profile Your Customers.....*4*
   The "5-Minute Marketing Plan".....*5*
   Winning the Loyalty of Your Existing Customers.....*6*
   Inactive Customers: "We Miss You!".....*7*
   New Customers: The Key to Growth.....*8*
   How to Find New Customers.....*9*

III. SALES STRATEGIES: Using Information to Sell Smarter
   How to Turn Your Sales Force into Tigers.....*11*
   Support Your Distribution Channel.....*13*
   How to Reduce Selling Costs and Improve Sales Productivity.....*16*

IV. THE POWER OF DIRECT MAIL
   "I Hate Direct Mail!"...THINK AGAIN!.....*17*
   A Sales Force of 255,000 Carriers.....*17*
   Direct Mail for Lead Generation.....*19*
   How to Sell with Direct Mail.....*21*
   Was Your Direct Mail Campaign a Failure? *Think Again. Maybe Not!*.....*23*
   Direct Mail "Do's and Don'ts".....*27*

V. THE POWER OF THE TELEPHONE
   Unleashing the Potential of Selling by Phone.....*29*
   "We Miss You!"-Call Your Inactive Customers.....*31*
   Qualifying Prospects to Cut Sales Costs.....*32*

VI. HOW DO WE COMPILE THE FINEST DATABASE OF 11 MILLION U.S. AND CANADIAN BUSINESSES
   We Start with the Best Basic Sources.....*33*
   Then We Make 14 Million Phone Calls.....*34*
   List Products.....*35*
   Directory Products.....*36*
   Electronic Products
      Magnetic Formats.....*37*
      On-Line Retrieval.....*37*
      CD-ROMS.....*38*
   InfoAccess Service.....*39*
   Non-Stop Sales Leads.....*40*

VII. CONCLUSION: We Want to Help You Find New Customers and Grow Your Business.....*41*

I. WHAT IS BUSINESS-TO-BUSINESS MARKETING?

In our daily lives, we are most familiar with Business-to-Consumer marketing. When we buy a box of cereal, a pair of jeans, a stereo, or a refrigerator, we are a part of Business-to-Consumer marketing. In fact, most of the advertising we see every day on television, read in newspapers, or hear on the radio is designed to sell products or services to consumers.

But there's another whole world of marketing out there -- involving the flow of goods from the manufacturer through the distribution channels to the retailer, who then sells them to you and me. This is called *Business-to-Business Marketing*.

Of the 10 million businesses in the U.S., over 3 million are involved in Business-to-Business Marketing. They include manufacturers, distributors, wholesalers, importers, manufacturers' representatives, and various companies who provide services to businesses. These companies work quietly behind the scenes to make products available to consumers.

CHALLENGES FACING BUSINESS-TO-BUSINESS MARKETERS

Business-to-business marketers cannot use the same methods as retailers in order to sell their products. Their market areas tend to be very broad, and yet there are a smaller number of potential customers. So the traditional consumer advertising media -- television, radio, billboards, and newspapers -- are not cost-effective.

Business-to-business marketers need a sharp focus in identifying potential customers in their market area, and then reaching them with their sales message. The key ingredient is INFORMATION -- an accurate database of information on businesses, which can be selected in ways to pinpoint potential customers.

The following chapters will build upon this overall theme -- **USING BUSINESS INFORMATION TO FIND NEW CUSTOMERS, REDUCE SELLING COSTS, IMPROVE MARKETING EFFICIENCY, AND INCREASE SALES AND PROFITS.**

II. THE FIRST STEP IN MARKETING...*Know Your Customers!*

Ask any business owner or sales manager what they know about their customers, and they'll say "Oh, I know all about them." But do they, really? When you ask, "How big is your average customer? How many employees do they have? What industries are they in?" -- that same business owner might scratch their head and realize how little they actually know about their customer base. And yet, that knowledge can be a "gold mine" for their business!

Every business-to-business marketer should know the basic "profile" of their customers -- who they are, what their needs are. Once you know the characteristics of your existing customers, it's much easier to find new **prospects.** In the next section, we'll talk about how you can develop a profile of your customers.

HOW TO PROFILE YOUR CUSTOMERS

"Profiling" is nothing more than learning more about your customers. Once you know their key characteristics, you'll be equipped to find more **new** customers. It's a simple concept, but one that's too often ignored.

To start putting your customer profile together, ask yourself the following questions:

1. *What types of businesses buy from me? What industries are they in?*

2. *How big are my customers? Are they mostly large corporations, or small "Mom and Pop" operations?*

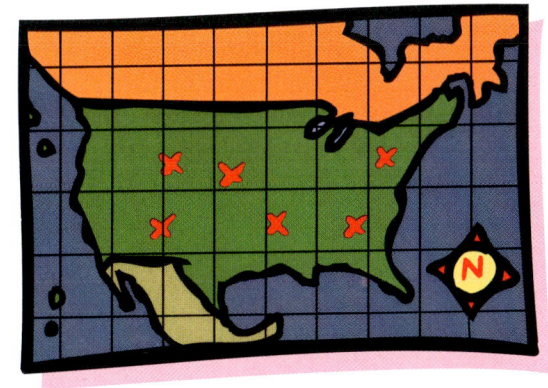

3. *Where are my customers located? In a regional sales territory, or all across the country? Are there any areas that have better potential than others?*

Once you have the answers to these questions, you'll be amazed how easy it is to zero in on the best potential customers for your business.

American Business Information, Inc. can help you, by performing a "Profile Analysis" of your customers. It's a simple process, and costs very little. Yet, it can be one of the most powerful tools you can have for acquiring new customers.

Here's how it works: we match your customer file against our database of 10 million businesses, and identify their characteristics. We can analyze them by SIC Code, Number of Employees, Sales Volume, or geographically by State, County, or ZIP Code. Then, we summarize the findings in an easy-to-use report that can really work wonders for your prospecting efforts.

Now that you've got a profile of your customers, what do you do? First, you need a **plan of attack**. In the next section, we'll talk about a simple framework you can use -- the "5-Minute Marketing Plan."

THE "5-MINUTE MARKETING PLAN"

With many things in life, the simplest ideas are often the best ones. Sam Walton believed following a simple, common sense approach is the key to success.

A marketing plan does not have to be lengthy and complicated. Instead, it should focus on the key elements for growing any business.

1. How to sell more to your existing customers.

2. How to find new customers

Our good friend and customer, Mr. Bob Hayes, is founder and Chairman of "Radio Engineering," an electronic component distributor. Bob has been using American Business Information, Inc.'s database for more than 15 years.

Bob uses a "5-minute Marketing Plan" -- a simple, effective approach to growing a business. Bob focuses his efforts on four basic groups: **large customers**, **active customers**, **inactive customers**, and **new customers**.

WINNING THE LOYALTY OF EXISTING CUSTOMERS

Too often, after we have spent a lot of time and effort to acquire a customer, we lose them because of neglect. It is **absolutely critical** to stay in touch with your existing customers, if you want to keep their loyalty.

Bob Hayes segments his customers into two groups: **large** customers, and **active** customers. Then, a separate contact strategy is used for each group.

Large customers get very special treatment. The sales staff contacts them every few weeks, and Bob calls them personally quite often. Plus, Bob visits them at least once a year, to "wine and dine them" and discuss their needs.

For **active customers**, Bob makes sure the sales staff is always in touch. They call at least once a month, and even visit most customers in person. Plus, a group of "telemarketing" representatives call them regularly to announce special offers, closeouts, and new products. And of course, Bob sends a catalog to active customers at least 6 times a year.

The point is to keep your name in front of your existing customers *all the time*. That way, they won't forget about you and go somewhere else!

INACTIVE CUSTOMERS: "We miss you!"

When a customer has not placed an order for over a year, they are considered "inactive." This raises a red flag with Bob Hayes; after investing a lot of money to acquire a new customer, he sure doesn't want to lose them.

So, a special group of Customer Service Representatives call the inactive customers to find out why they stopped buying. If the customer is upset, they try to smooth things over. And, sometimes Bob calls the inactive customers himself to get their feedback.

The whole idea is to find out why these customers stopped buying, and do whatever is necessary to get them back. It's a strategy that pays dividends!

WHAT EVER HAPPENED TO ACME? THEY USED TO BE A GOOD CLIENT...

NEW CUSTOMERS: The Key to Growth

No matter how well you service your existing customers, you are bound to lose some of them sooner or later. They might go out of business, or simply stop handling your type of products. And in these cases, there's nothing you can do to keep them.

The solution is obvious: find more **new customers** to replace the ones lost due to attrition. This is where American Business Information, Inc. helps Bob Hayes and Radio Engineering in their growth strategy.

HOW TO FIND NEW CUSTOMERS

First, Bob uses a **Customer Profile Analysis** (discussed in the last section) to identify prospective customers by type of business (or SIC Code) and number of employees. Then, he orders a **"Sales Lead Package"** of these prospects on **3" x 5" cards**, **prospecting lists**, **mailing labels**, and **diskettes**.

CUSTOMER PROFILE

SIZE: 500 em
TYPE of BUSIN
SIC CODE:

SALES LEAD CARDS

ABC CORP
1334 W. APPLE ROAD
RICHMOND, VA 23230
123145623
PAUL JONES
804/078-7869
FAX 804-907-8594
OWNER
4399-79 COMPUTER SOFTWARE DUPL
91   A
$1 MILLION-$1.5 MILLION
GENDER: MALE

The **3" x 5" cards** are divided by sales territory and given to the sales staff for prospecting. They qualify the leads, and call on the better potentials. It's a great way to sign up new customers. And our **Credit Rating Codes** allow the sales staff to determine the credit worthiness of potential customers.

MAILING LABELS / DISKETTES

Mailing labels are used to send a catalog to prospects six times a year. With each mailing, there is a special offer on a particular product. For example, when Bob ran a special on "surge protectors," he sold them by the truckload!

Also, the **diskettes** are loaded onto the sales automation software on their PC network. It can then be used for invoicing, personalized mailings, and follow-up.

PROSPECT LISTS

On top of this, Bob's telemarketing staff uses the **prospecting lists** to call potential customers about the monthly special. This works very well as a follow-up to the mailing.

The bottom line is this: Bob Hayes and Radio Engineering are successful because they try to find new customers every way they can. And with American Business Information, Inc.'s help, they succeed.

©AMERICAN BUSINESS INFORMATION, INC.
5711 S. 86th Cir. • P.O. Box 27347 • Omaha, NE 68127
Phone (402) 592-9000 • Fax (402) 331-1505

III. SALES STRATEGIES: Using Information to Sell Smarter

Maintaining a sales force today is very expensive. A good salesperson's time is worth over $200 an hour -- so they can't waste that precious time scrambling to find prospects. They must spend every hour in front of customers, **selling**.

How to Turn Your Sales Force into Tigers

Just think of the tiger in the jungle. If he had no idea where his prey might be, he would quickly starve to death. But the tiger has **information** -- on where the water holes and trails are -- that helps him locate his dinner more quickly. And that's exactly what a salesperson must do: use information on prospects to avoid hunting in the wrong places.

It all boils down to knowing more about your potential customers. The more information you have, the easier it is to find your target. And that's where American Business Information, Inc. can help. Our database can provide the information your sales force needs to be more efficient, productive hunters.

A "Customer Profile Analysis" (from the last chapter) can help you pinpoint who your best potential customers are. Or, maybe you already know your market quite well. Either way, **use** that knowledge by **providing leads to your salespeople**. Give them the tools they need to stalk their prey efficiently.

One quick phone call to American Business Information, Inc. is all it takes to order thousands of new leads for your sales force -- for only a few pennies per lead. Our 3"x5" Sales Lead Cards are a convenient way to distribute the leads among your salespeople. Or, you can order diskettes to load into your sales management software.

Once your salespeople have the leads, you may need to make sure they **work** them initially. Not every lead will turn into a customer, of course. But as they close more and more of the leads, they'll turn into a sales force of "tigers."

Support Your Distribution Channel
Help Your Distributors and Manufacturers' Reps

Many business-to-business marketers use **distributors** and **manufacturers reps**, who play an important role in the channel of distribution for goods and services.

While these sales "partners" are an essential part of the marketing process, too often the manufacturers ignore them. They think that once they sign up a distributor, or manufacturers' rep, or dealer network, then they can go to sleep and do nothing. But those distributors, reps, or dealers may be selling products for **20 other companies**. How do you make sure they are selling as much of *your* products as possible?

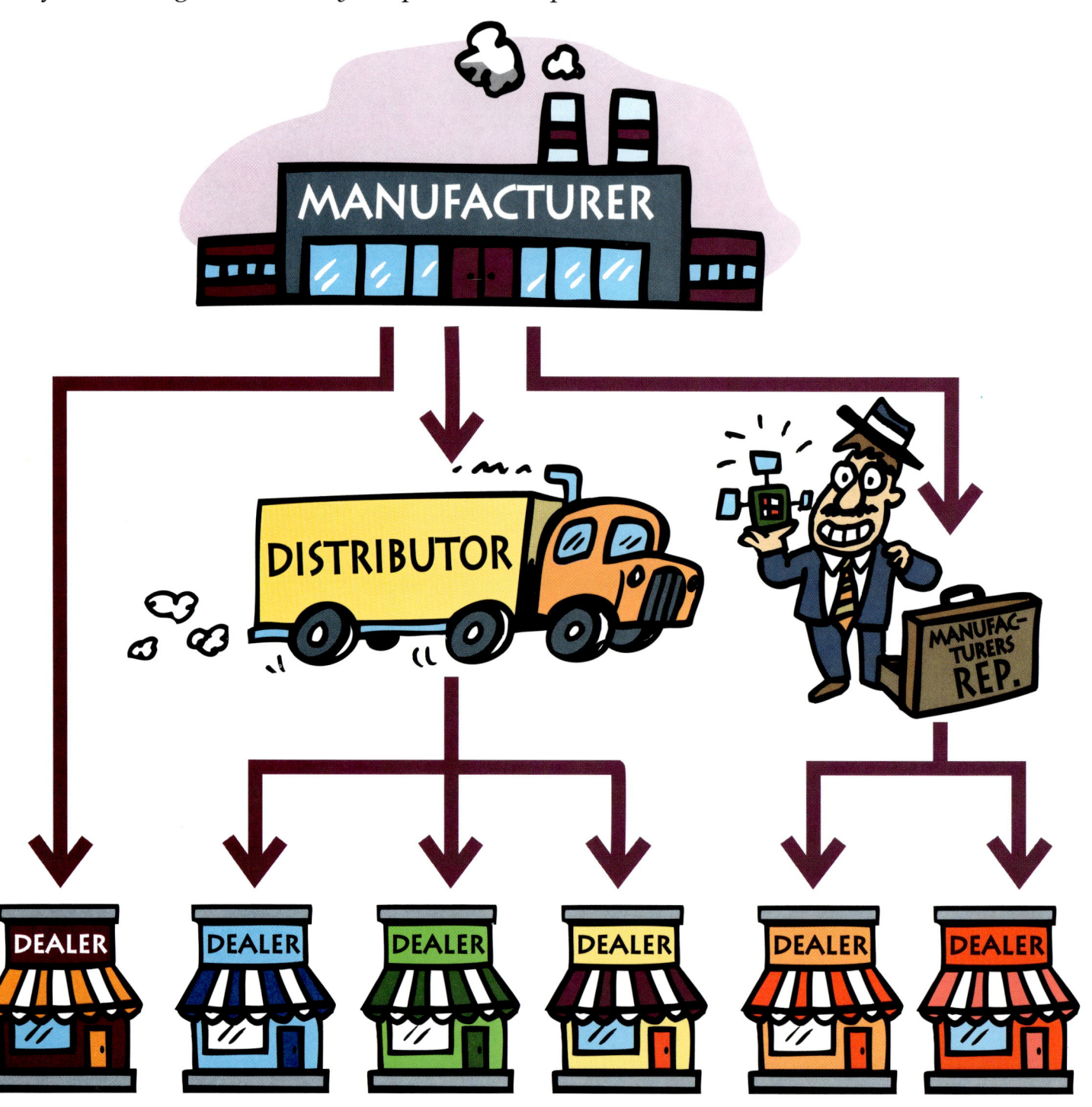

The answer is simple: if you want your distributors, dealers, or reps to be loyal to you and sell more of your products, **you have to help them**. How? By giving them the support they need to sell more efficiently, just like you would for your own sales force.

1. Profile their customers. Our Customer Profile Analysis is ideal for new dealers, distributors, or reps. It can help you show them how to prospect for new customers who will buy your products.

2. Provide Them with Sales Leads. Once you have the profile, you can provide lists of potential customers to each distributor, rep, or dealer. Their sales force will then be more productive in selling your products.

American Business Information, Inc. can help accomplish this by setting up **Dealer Programs** for you. We keep track of the sales territories for each of your resellers, and provide leads to them on a regular basis. Dealer Programs are a very effective way to keep the loyalty of your distribution channel partners.

3. Advertise for Them. You can use direct mail advertising to promote your product to the potential customers of your distributors, and have them contact the distributors for orders. This is an economical way to generate leads for your distributors; the cost is usually very small, but the programs generate tremendous loyalty from your distributors, reps, or dealers.

Always remember: your distributors, manufacturers reps, and dealers are your "outside sales force." If you want them to move more product, you must keep them happy and help them by supporting their sales efforts. When you do, they'll be "tigers" working for you!

How to Reduce Selling Costs and Improve Sales Productivity

By now you have probably noticed a common theme, for the sales force **and** distribution channel partners -- **help them sell smarter.** It boils down to a simple two-step approach:

1. HELP THE SALESPEOPLE IDENTIFY WHO THE POTENTIAL CUSTOMERS ARE.

2. PROVIDE LEADS OF THOSE POTENTIAL CUSTOMERS TO THEM, REGULARLY.

It doesn't matter whether it's your own sales force, or that of your distributors or reps -- the effect is the same. They will spend their time more productively with this approach, and they'll sell more at a lower cost. And everybody wins, from the manufacturer down to the ultimate consumer.

American Business Information, Inc. can provide all the tools you need to reduce your selling costs and improve sales productivity. Just call, and we'll help you.

©AMERICAN BUSINESS INFORMATION, INC.
5711 S. 86th Cir. • P.O. Box 27347 • Omaha, NE 68127
Phone (402) 592-9000 • Fax (402) 331-1505

IV. THE POWER OF DIRECT MAIL

"I Hate Direct Mail!"...THINK AGAIN! Be honest...do you really hate advertising mail? Chances are you yourself have ordered something from a mail order catalog in the past year! And for business-to-business marketing, direct mail is the most economical way to communicate your message to a targeted audience.

A Sales Force of 255,000 Carriers. The U.S. Postal Service is an incredibly efficient way to deliver a printed message. It's a model for the entire world. And those 255,000 mail carriers can act as your sales force, in those times when it's not possible to send a salesperson to call on a potential customer.

Just think about the costs. It can cost $300 for a face-to-face sales call, in a **local** market. If the call is out of town, it can be much more. But the mail carrier will deliver your sales message for less than a dollar, in most cases.

Direct mail advertising is a huge industry. In fact, more money is spent on direct mail than **any other** form of advertising. In this section, we will talk about how you can use direct mail effectively, and put those 255,000 "salespeople" to work for you.

Direct Mail for Lead Generation

In the last chapter, we talked about using the traditional methods of distribution - a sales force, distributors, reps, and dealers - to sell products. Direct mail can be a very effective way to help this process, by generating leads for the salespeople. In fact, direct mail is probably the most economical way of all to generate qualified leads.

How do you do it? The first step is knowing **who to mail to**. A profile of your potential customers, as we have discussed, can be very helpful here. Or, you can call us and we'll discuss the various lists available.

Next, **what do you mail?** Lead generation mailings are usually very simple, since they are designed to get people interested, but **not** to "make the sale." There are two types of "packages" that are commonly used:

- **An envelope mailing:** typically this includes a sales letter, a brochure or flyer describing the product, and a card to be filled out and sent back for more information. This is the "lead" that goes to the salesperson.

- ***A self-mailer:*** often a simple brochure that requires no envelope and costs less to produce. It is usually printed on heavier paper, and has a perforated reply card to be sent back.

In both cases, the purpose of a lead generation mailing is to get people interested enough to call or send back the reply card. The message should include some kind of offer, so they will call or write quickly.

Once a lead comes back in, it is very important to follow up on it **right away**, before the prospect has a chance to "cool off" or forgets what your product was. Many programs fail because the leads don't get followed up. Make sure you have a system to get leads to the salespeople quickly, and make sure they follow up while the leads are fresh.

How to Sell with Direct Mail

Selling products with direct mail is a multi-billion-dollar industry, involving thousands of companies who use catalogs to sell their products. It's **different** than lead generation mailings, because it's a "one-step" approach that does not require a sales visit to close the order. Direct mail selling is used for small-ticket items, or products that are familiar to the customers and will be ordered without salespeople having to "pitch" them. They simply call up, usually on an "800" number, and place their order.

In order to sell products through the mail, the catalog or mailer must contain more product information than a lead generation mailing. You should give the customer all the facts needed to make a buying decision, so that they can simply call or write to order. Also, a satisfaction guarantee will help generate more orders by giving the customer more confidence.

More and more businesses order products by mail today, because of the convenience. It takes less of their time to order from a mail-order company than to deal with a salesperson, and often they can get a better price. Direct mail selling could represent a great opportunity for you, as well.

Was Your Direct Mail Campaign a Failure?
Think Again. Maybe Not!

Once you start looking into direct mail, and reading the literature, talking to people... you will hear some **"myths"** that can be very misleading. Here are a few you should be careful about:

MYTH 1: *"You should get at least a 1% response, or the mailing was bad."*

Have you heard this one? The fact is, response rate alone does not tell you whether a mailing was successful. What matters is, **did you make money?** You need to look at the return on your investment in the mailing. Here's a simple example:

> Average order = $1000
> Your margin is 40%
> Gross Profit per order = $400
>
> Cost of mailing = 40¢ per piece
> (including printing, postage, mailing service)

Now -- let's look at the numbers and get a **true** picture of this mailing:

> To mail 1,000 pieces, your cost is: $400
>
> Assume you get 4 orders: Gross Profit is $1600
>
> Your return on investment is 4.0 times: you <u>quadrupled your money</u>, in gross profit. Was this mailing a success? You would probably say, "<u>yes</u>".
>
> Percent Response=4/1000=0.4%

As this example shows, just looking at the percent response is not enough. The "1% Response Myth" came from consumer mailings, where the average order size was $20-30. In business-to-business mailings, the larger average order means that a lower response rate can still be very profitable.

MYTH 2: *"I got back over 100 'undeliverables' on my 2000-piece mailing. That list was terrible!"*

Was it? Let's face the facts: lists are not perfect. In this case, the undeliverable rate was about 5% -- which is really quite **good**. Think about all the changes in the business world every day. It's simply impossible to maintain 100% deliverability on **any** business list.

Once, I asked a customer who complained about the undeliverables, "But did you get any orders?"

He paused, then replied: "Well, yes, I got a **lot** of orders. I spent about $1000 on the mailing, and we have almost $20,000 in orders so far."

Then, when I asked that customer if he still thought the list was terrible, he laughed... and placed another order!

The point is simple: judge a list by the **results**. Did you get orders, did you generate enough leads? Undeliverables are a fact of life -- don't let them take your attention away from the real issue. If the list got the desired results, it was a good list...despite the undeliverables.

MYTH 3: *"I sent out 1500 mailers and only got 20 calls. That list didn't work"*

In this case, we need to focus on the **purpose** of the mailing. Was it designed to generate inquiries, or orders? What is the average order size? What is the typical close rate on inquiries?

In this example: let's assume the sales force will close 20% of those 20 calls within 3 months. That's only 4 new customers. **BUT** -- what if an average customer spends over $10,000 per year, and you have a 30% profit margin? Those 4 new customers are worth **$12,000 in profit** -- all from a 1500-piece mailing.

Again, it's easy to be misled if you don't work the numbers. A simple cost/benefit analysis can tell you whether that mailing was a success, or a failure.

Direct Mail "Do's and Don'ts"

American Business Information, Inc. mails out about 30 million pieces of mail each year -- we really "practice what we preach" in our own marketing efforts. And over the years, we have learned a few things about direct mail advertising that we'd like to pass along. Here are some basic "do's and don'ts":

DO:

- **Keep your message simple.** You have only a few seconds to get your prospects' attention -- do it with a simple, powerful message that clearly tells what you're selling, and the benefits. Avoid too many details, especially on the cover of a brochure.

- **Test.** Many variables can affect the response to a mailing; the list, the offer, price, and so forth. Test with smaller mailings -- a few thousand pieces -- to refine these variables before rolling out those big mailings. This can help you prevent major mistakes.

- **Analyze the response.** Make sure you can track leads and orders, so you can determine the return on your mailing investment.

- **Mail more than once.** Repetition is important; mail at least six times a year to your prospects for maximum impact.

DON'T:

- **Mail only once.** Too many times, businesses use a mailing as a one-time "knee jerk" reaction when things are slow. But this doesn't give a true picture of the potential. Like other kinds of advertising, repetition is the key to success in direct mail. You should mail at least six times to the same group to get best results.

- **Forget existing customers.** Direct mail is a great way to stay in touch with your customers, offer them specials, and get more orders from them. You should mail to existing customers several times a year.

There are many good "How-to" books on direct mail advertising on the market. For further information, contact the Direct Marketing Association at 404/664-7284 and ask for their "Publications Catalog." Or write:

Direct Marketing Association
Book Distribution Center
1650 Bluegrass Lakes Parkway
Alpharetta, GA 30201

V. THE POWER OF THE TELEPHONE

There's something "magical" about the telephone. For just about everyone, when the phone rings we grab it. And in a selling situation, the phone is a personal, persuasive way to deliver a message. You can use your personality and charm to get your point across, and interact with your customer to answer questions and objections.

Just think of the amount of business you conduct over the phone, every day. It's the most powerful communication medium...when you can't be there in person.

Unleashing the Potential of Selling by Phone

Telephone sales is used by virtually every business-to-business marketer in the country today...especially with the skyrocketing costs of a face-to-face sales call. However, getting the maximum benefit from telephone sales requires a disciplined and well-organized approach.

Inbound Tele-Sales -- is a very cost-effective way to take orders generated from a direct mail campaign, space ads, or other advertising. To achieve optimum results, here are some tips:

- ***Answer the Phone Quickly*** -- Customers should not have to listen to more than 3 rings, and should be able to talk with your representative with a minimum of transfers.

- ***Train the "Order-Takers" to Sell*** -- You spend a lot of advertising dollars to generate a phone inquiry... to maximize your efforts, the customer representatives need to **close** a high percentage of those inquiries. Basic sales training for your inbound reps will pay dividends.

- ***Go After "Add-On" Sales*** -- When a customer calls and orders one item, **don't stop there**. Ask about their needs, offer specials, try to sell them some additional products.

Outbound Tele-Sales -- can result in a dramatic improvement in market penetration and overall sales productivity. Outbound sales calls are especially effective as a "follow-up" to direct mail campaigns, and work particularly well with existing customers. Here's some "nuts and bolts" advice:

- ***Hire "tigers"*** -- Outbound tele-sales requires a more aggressive, better-trained sales person than inbound order-taking. Don't expect good results from timid types -- find reps with the "killer instinct" and work to develop their sales techniques.

- ***"Work the Numbers"*** -- To a large extent, outbound tele-sales is a "numbers game." The rep who makes 100 calls a day will almost always outsell the one who makes 50 calls. Monitor the salespeople, help them weed out the non-productive calls quicker, and keep them **dialing**. It will pay off.

©AMERICAN BUSINESS INFORMATION, INC.
5711 S. 86th Cir. • P.O. Box 27347 • Omaha, NE 68127
Phone (402) 592-9000 • Fax (402) 331-1505

"WE MISS YOU!" -- Call Your Inactive Customers

When a customer stops buying from you and becomes inactive, it's time to take action. The telephone is the ideal way to contact these inactive customers. It's definitely worth the efforts to avoid losing the initial investment you made in getting them as customers. Yet, this activity is too often overlooked.

Call your inactive customers, and find out why they stopped buying. They'll tell you what went wrong -- and this feedback can help you improve your product, adjust your pricing, beef up your customer service...**fix** the problem.

Use a special, highly-trained group of representatives for these calls, and **listen** to your inactive customers. Often there was a simple misunderstanding, or a small problem that's easy to resolve. You can often get them back, if you make the effort. If you don't, they are gone for good!

Qualifying Prospects to Cut Sales Costs

With today's emphasis on improving sales efficiency and reducing selling costs, **prospect qualification** is becoming the rule, rather than the exception. Many business-to-business marketers have established telephone lead qualification centers, to supply the field sales offices with highly-qualified potential customers. This results in much better sales productivity.

We have explored just a few ways in which the power of the telephone can enhance your sales and marketing efforts. And, American Business Information, Inc. can assist you with a **100% telephone-verified** database of 10 million businesses. We use the phone quite a bit ourselves -- making **14 million** phone calls every year to verify our database.

In the next section, you will learn how our database is compiled, how we can deliver it to you, and how it can fit into the strategies we have discussed for finding new customers.

©AMERICAN BUSINESS INFORMATION, INC.
5711 S. 86th Cir. • P.O. Box 27347 • Omaha, NE 68127
Phone (402) 592-9000 • Fax (402) 331-1505

VI. HOW DO WE COMPILE THE FINEST DATABASE OF 11 MILLION U.S. AND CANADIAN BUSINESSES

The American Business Information, Inc. database is the most complete and accurate source of business information for sales, marketing and credit applications. Creating this database requires a staff of over 330 full-time employees, who update and verify the information on a continuous, real-time basis. Here's how we do it...

We Start with the Best Basic Sources. Over the years, we have evaluated the hundreds of different sources of business data, and have chosen only the very best and most reliable ones for our database. They include:

- Yellow Pages and Business White Pages
- Annual Reports, 10-K's and other SEC Information
- Federal, State and Municipal Government Data
- Leading Business Magazines, Newsletters, and Major Newspapers
- Postal Service Information: NCOA, ZIP+4 and Carrier Route Files
- Bankruptcy Records and Legal Filings

These sources help us identify virtually every business in the U.S. and Canada.

Then We Make 14 Million Phone Calls.
Even though we use the most reliable sources available, the information does not go into our database until it's verified by our telephone research staff. There is simply no better way to ensure the accuracy of our data. Yes, it's expensive...but we think your satisfaction is well worth the investment.

By actually calling all 11 million businesses every year (and more often for larger companies), we can keep up with the tremendous amount of change that occurs. We confirm addresses and phone numbers, weed out companies who have gone out of business, and collect additional information: **Name of the Owner or Key Decision-Maker, Number of Employees, Primary Line of Business,** and more. Our telephone verification process is what sets our database apart from our competitors.

Finally...Credit Rating Codes. In response to overwhelming demand from customers, we have developed Credit Rating Codes for most of the businesses in our database. We consider business demographics and historical performance information and use a sophisticated multivariate-regression model to determine probable credit worthiness of businesses. These codes make our database more useful for credit and marketing applications.

The End Result: The Best Database of 11 Million Businesses Ever Created. In terms of completeness, accuracy, and depth of information, no other source can compare to our database. Our commitment to quality at every level of the compilation effort guarantees you the best business marketing information available.

©AMERICAN BUSINESS INFORMATION, INC.
5711 S. 86th Cir. • P.O. Box 27347 • Omaha, NE 68127
Phone (402) 592-9000 • Fax (402) 331-1505

LIST

Prospect Lists

These easy-to-read single line listings are perfect for sales planning, telemarketing, or following up on inquiries. Each Prospect List is individually printed on a laser printer for maximum legibility.

Prospect Lists may be ordered in three different sequences at no additional charge.

By City. This sequence is ordered most often.
By County. Useful if sales territories are set up on a county basis.
By ZIP Code. This sequence is preferred when ordered along with mailing labels. The matching sequence makes it easier to follow-up on the mailing.
By Walk Sequence. Great for sales people selling door-to-door.

Mailing Labels

Standard size labels are laser-printed four-up in ZIP Code sequence to facilitate bulk mailings. Other sequences are available upon request. You may order Pressure Sensitive (peel-off) Labels, or ungummed Cheshire Labels for mailing house use. Our mailing labels do not include phone numbers. We can print phone numbers if requested.

Name of the Owner or Manager is available for most of our business names at an additional charge. These key contacts can improve your results, whether you are using direct mail or telemarketing.

Sales Lead Cards

Our 3 x 5 Sales Lead Cards are the ideal format for prospect card files or telemarketing "calling cards". You can order any of the sequences available for the Prospect List above.

DIRECTORY

Our directory division, American Business Directories, produces a wide range of business directories to meet the needs of businesses. Six different lines of directories are published:

Business Credit Reference Directory. The nation's most convenient resource for business credit information. This unique, 12-volume set provides credit rating codes (valuable for credit, qualifying new customers, suppliers and other applications) for nearly 10 million U.S. companies. The directory is also available on CD-ROM and is accessible through ONLINE services, and through our toll free 800 number.

State Business Directories. Every business in a state is listed and arranged by "type of business" or by "city" in these directories. They're designed for companies whose market area is limited to a state or two.

Directories by SIC. These directories are designed for companies that market to particular industries, such as car dealers, computer dealers, pet shops or physicians, to name a few. More than 2,000 different directories are available, covering virtually every type of business.

Manufacturers Directory. Manufacturing firms comprise a huge segment of the U.S. economy, spending in excess of a trillion dollars annually on raw materials, equipment and services. American Business Information, Inc. publishes a nationwide directory of 120,000 top manufacturers, which is ideal for companies that market their products or services to manufacturers.

Big Business Directory. Big businesses still account for the majority of spending, making this directory a valuable source for general purpose reference and marketing needs. It contains 140,000 top U.S. companies with 100 or more employees, and includes 276,000 key executives and directors.

Metro Area Business Directories. The Company's "Contacts Influential" division has been a leader in business directory publishing for more than 22 years. These directories are comprehensive sales and marketing guides to businesses in a city, and include in-depth information on each company listed. Directories are available for 18 major metropolitan areas.

©AMERICAN BUSINESS INFORMATION, INC.
5711 S. 86th Cir. • P.O. Box 27347 • Omaha, NE 68127
Phone (402) 592-9000 • Fax (402) 331-1505

ELECTRONIC PRODUCTS

Magnetic Formats

Magnetic Tape: Available on ASCII or EBCDIC (IBM) machine languages, 1600 or 6250 BPI. We can provide any blocking factor desired and any sequence.

PC Diskettes: are IBM-PC (5 1/4" & 3 1/2"), IBM-3740 (8"), Apple IIe (5 1/4") or Apple Macintosh (3 1/2") compatible.

Mailing List Software: **My MailList**™ (by MySoftware Company) provides the easiest way to manage mailing lists. The software package will generate mailing labels and reports, sort by any field, and allow addition, correction or deletion of individual records. **My MailList**™ software will run on any IBM-PC compatible system. **It is offered free with any diskette order.**

Cartridge Tape: Available on 3480 cartridges for mainframe computers, or PC based cartridges.

On-Line Retrieval

Imagine being able to tap into a database of 11 million businesses whenever you want, 24 hours a day, to retrieve and qualify prospects for your business. It's easy --with American Business Lists - ONLINE. All you need is a PC and a modem.

SELECT LISTINGS BY:
- SIC Code or Yellow Page Category
- Number of Employees
- Estimated Sales Volume
- Contact Name or Title
  ...for any geographic area!

PLUS -- Now Includes **Credit Rating Codes!**

American Business Lists - Online is an instant source of information for Sales Leads, Direct Marketing, Market Research, Making Credit Decisions, and more.

Business America - ON CD-ROM

How Does Business America - ON CD-ROM Work? We provide you with everything you need to set up your own Marketing Workstation, complete with PC and CD-ROM drive. All 10 million businesses are contained on one CD-ROM and our easy-to-use retrieval software allows maximum flexibility for your searches -- at incredible speeds! After only a couple of sessions, you'll be performing searches and printing information with ease! If you don't need hardware -- no problem, we can provide the base system only.

Every listing includes: company name, full address & telephone, key contact name and title, SIC codes, stock exchange and ticker symbol on public companies, credit rating codes, number of employees, annual sales volume, and headquarter/branch identifiers.

With **Business America - ON CD-ROM'S** unique record key system, you'll have unlimited screen-viewing of the company name, city, state, and line of business profile. When you need complete information such as full address & telephone, SIC Code, key contact names, number of employees -- the record key "counts" only what you print or download from the disc. No other desktop marketing product allows you this type of flexibility right on your PC!

American Yellow Pages - ON CD-ROM

Now there's a single source for information on any business in the U.S. The American Yellow Pages - on CD-ROM is the ultimate desktop business reference tool. You can call up a complete company profile which includes: Company Name, Complete Address, Telephone, SIC Codes & Yellow Page Descriptions and Franchise/Specialty Information. Up to 10 profiles can be selected at a time for printing and downloading. It even dials the phone numbers for you!

Search by:

    Type of Business -- using Yellow Page Heading or SIC Code.

    Company Name -- even if you don't know where they're located.

    Geographically -- by City, State, County, ZIP Code or total U.S.

©AMERICAN BUSINESS INFORMATION, INC.
5711 S. 86th Cir. • P.O. Box 27347 • Omaha, NE 68127
Phone (402) 592-9000 • Fax (402) 331-1505

INFOACCESS

"When You Need Business Information *Pronto* . . . Call 1-800-808-INFO!"

There are many times you need information when you're traveling, at a party, or just on the go. Yet, in this complex information age, when we need to find the right piece of business information, it's often impossible to get.

What if you could get the information you need, when you need it, right over the phone? **InfoAccess** was developed to meet this demand. We offer seven different services which are essential to every business. Our services include:

Company Profiles. Obtain facts and background information on public and private businesses.

Business Credit Reports. Payment history and public record information to help you make those tough credit decisions.

Business Directory Assistance. Helps you locate businesses when the "Phone Company Directory Assistance" can't help.

"Find-a-Person". Track down a friend, relative or business associate with this nationwide database.

Quick Research Service. Use the service to find the "sales growth rate of frozen yogurt in California" or "track down company quarterly or annual reports."

Business News Network. Find articles about virtually any company or topic, from more than 2,000 newspapers, magazines and newsletters.

Fax-a-List. Whether you need information for a quick prospect list, or simply a personal list to assist you in your vacation plans, Fax-a-List gets you the information you need when you need it.

NON-STOP SALES LEADS

What is the "Non-Stop Sales Leads" Program? It's an annual subscription plan that provides you with sales leads, on a continuous basis throughout the entire year. This program is designed to help you find new customers and increase your sales, month after month and year after year.

How Does It Work? First, we will profile your customers to determine their characteristics. This **Customer Profile Analysis** will show your best prospects by SIC Code and Employee Size. It becomes the basis for identifying your sales leads.

Once you know the number of prospects, we will provide you with the leads in the following formats every six months:

- A hard-copy **Prospect List**
- Two sets of **Mailing Labels**
- One set of 3 x 5 **Sales Lead Cards**
- And on **Diskettes** for your PC

And...New Leads Every Month! As we update our database each month, you will receive the **New Sales Leads** on 3 x 5 cards.

How Can I Use This Program? We have over 400,000 customers who use our...

- **Prospect List** to help their distributors, sales force, or reps for sales lead generation.

- **Mailing Labels** for direct mail campaigns. (You will get 4 sets of labels in a year, i.e. you can have 4 campaigns per year.)

- **Sales Lead Cards** for your telemarketing or field salespeople.

- **Diskettes** to set up a "Sales Automation" database system on your PC.

What Does the Program Cost? Much less than you might think! We will perform the **Customer Profile Analysis** at no charge, and you will pay only "pocket change" for each lead you receive. Exact pricing will vary, depending on the number of leads we identify for your market area.

How Do I Get Started? Just call Traci Duren or Doug Parsonage at (402) 593-4525 and you can get started right away.

WE WANT TO HELP YOU FIND NEW CUSTOMERS AND GROW YOUR BUSINESS!

For more information on any of our products or services, call (402) 592-9000.

Our Family of Companies:

- American Business Lists®
- American Business Directories
- BMI AMERICAN MEDICAL INFORMATION
- Ci CONTACTS INFLUENTIAL
- American Business Marketing
- American Business Communications
- Compilers plus
- INFO ACCESS
- Zeller List Corp.